OLIVER CREIGHTON AND ROBERT HIGHAM

G000061590

MEDIEVAL CASTLES

SHIRE ARCHAEOLOGY

Dedicated to the memories of two of the twentieth century's most influential castle scholars: R. Allen Brown and A. J. Taylor.

Cover illustration:
Stokesay Castle in Shropshire. One of the first fortified manor houses in England, it was built in the late thirteenth century.

British Library Cataloguing in Publication Data:
Creighton, Oliver.
Medieval castles. – (Shire archaeology; 83)
1. Castles – England – History – To 1500
2. Castles – Wales – History – To 1500
3. Architecture, Medieval – England
4. Architecture, Medieval – Wales
I. Title II. Higham, Robert
728.8'1'0942'0902.
ISBN-10 0 7478 0546 6.

Published by Shire Publications Ltd.
PO Box 883, Oxford, OX1 9PL, UK
PO Box 3985, New York, NY 10185-3985, USA
Email: shire@shirebooks.co.uk   www.shirebooks.co.uk

© 2003 Oliver Creighton and Robert Higham.

First published 2003.
Transferred to digital print on demand 2015.

Oliver Creighton and Robert Higham are hereby identified as the authors of this work in accordance with Section 77 of the Copyright, Designs and Patents Act, 1988.

Shire Archaeology series no. 83 • ISBN-13 978 0 74780 546 5.

Series Editor: James Dyer.

Printed and bound in Great Britain

Shire Publications is supporting the Woodland Trust, the UK's leading woodland conservation charity, by funding the dedication of trees.

Contents

4

List of illustrations

Acknowledgements

In addition to our debt to numerous colleagues who have given permission for the reproduction of illustrations (see below), we are also indebted in a wider sense to the communities of historians and archaeologists upon whose published efforts the compilation of this little book has so heavily depended. Our major challenge as authors has been one of compression, for the number and variety of castle sites that have received serious study is simply too large to be treated uniformly within the constraints of this publication. We are conscious, therefore, that our selection of places to discuss and of observations to make may not have been the selection that others would have made. We hope, however, that our choice of material gives a representative view of the extent and richness of castles and castle studies. While we hope our remarks illuminate the wider world of castles, our selection (including 'Sites to visit') has been largely from England and Wales.

We thank the following for granting permission to reproduce illustrations: *Archaeological Journal*; Clwyd-Powys Archaeological Trust; J. Coad; Exeter Archaeology; S. Goddard; Historic Scotland; Q. Hughes; R. Morris; National Monuments Record Centre, Swindon; Pipe Roll Society; C. Platt; M. Rouillard; A. D. Saunders; P. Scholefield.

National Grid References are used with the permission of the Controller of Her Majesty's Stationery Office.

1
Introduction: castles and castle studies

On the modern Ordnance Survey map, the word 'castle' will be found attached to many different sorts of site, ranging from prehistoric hillforts to post-medieval houses of the gentry. This loose use of the word can sometimes cause confusion about what castles really were. Though some of its characteristics were found in earlier and later centuries, to the archaeologist and historian the castle was a phenomenon of the medieval period, built in England and Wales broadly from the eleventh to the fifteenth century. Its essential character was an amalgamation of several diverse qualities. Castles were defensible. They were private homes. They were also normally centres of administration and symbols of a social élite that wielded immense power and wealth.

The English word 'castle' comes from the Latin *castellum*, the diminutive of *castrum,* meaning 'fortification'. This Latin word gave rise to the Old English *castel*, in addition to a range of European vernacular forms, including *château* (from *chastel*, French), *castillo* (Spanish) and *castello* (Italian). Curiously, one of the English words most commonly associated by the public with castles is 'keep' (figure 1). This word, however, was not in common usage in the medieval period. Instead, the type of building with which the word 'keep' is

1. The royal donjon of Scarborough Castle, North Yorkshire (commenced 1158), as depicted by George Clark in *Mediaeval Military Architecture in England*, volume 2, 1884. Outwardly an austere building, this structure nevertheless has fine Romanesque details.

2. Dover Castle, Kent. Described as 'the key of England' by the thirteenth-century chronicler Matthew Paris, this famous royal castle occupies a site whose defensive qualities had been recognised over one thousand years earlier by the builders of the Iron Age hillfort in which it stands. (Photograph: the authors)

usually associated was known to contemporaries as *magna turris* (in Latin), or as *donjon* (Anglo-Norman French). The word 'donjon' derived from the Latin *dominium*, meaning 'lordship', underlining the social symbolism inherent in these great buildings. Although the prehistoric, Roman and post-medieval sites to which the word 'castle' is often applied sometimes shared these defensive and domestic characteristics, the defining quality of the medieval castle was that it displayed these many attributes simultaneously. Due allowance must be made, however, for differing emphasis within particular medieval castles. Thus at one end of the spectrum, medieval royal fortresses such as the Tower of London and Dover Castle (Kent) represent the height of royal power, prestige and investment, and the pinnacle of contemporary military and domestic sophistication (figure 2). At the opposite end of the spectrum, many of the smallest castles were little more than defensible estate centres built by the lords of rural manors. Good examples of these types of site are the motte and bailey castles at Parracombe (Devon) and Hallaton (Leicestershire), both built as the power bases of local Norman lords holding scatters of rural estates in their localities (figure 3). Despite their differences, these four sites co-existed in the twelfth century and together illustrate the common aspiration of rich medieval people to display their strength and status through private fortification.

3. Holwell Castle, Parracombe, Devon. The grassed-over earthworks of this small motte and bailey represent one of the numerous earth-and-timber castles erected by Norman lords in the late eleventh and early twelfth centuries. (Photograph: the authors)

Castles have been studied in various ways since the sixteenth century. Antiquarians from John Leland onwards took a keen interest in the ancestral homes of the rich and powerful. This study of castles as reflections of aristocratic culture continued to be popular until the later nineteenth century (figure 4). By this time, however, historians were pursuing more sophisticated and rigorous approaches to the study of the medieval period, which had a secondary impact on other emerging disciplines. Studies of ecclesiastical architecture had also advanced in the earlier part of the nineteenth century and from these foundations grew a more mature approach to the study of secular buildings. Particularly significant developments in this field were the publication

4. Caerphilly Castle, Glamorgan, as depicted by Samuel and Nathaniel Buck in 1740. This is one of their numerous illustrations of historic buildings.

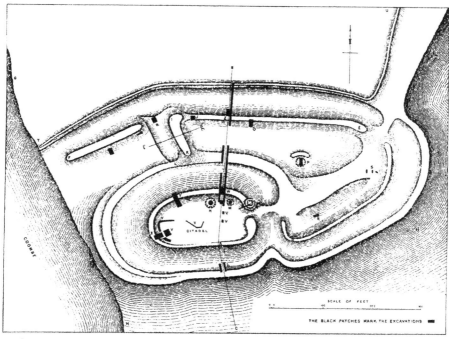

5. Caesar's Camp, Folkestone, Kent, as depicted in General Pitt Rivers's report on his excavations (published in *Archaeologia*, 47, 1883). Although its site name reflects a Roman ascription in the antiquarian tradition, the excavation revealed the site to be a medieval castle.

of J. Parker's famous survey of this subject, *Some Account of the Domestic Architecture in England from Edward I to Richard II* (1882), and George Clark's seminal *Mediaeval Military Architecture in England* (1884). At the same time, archaeologists were beginning to address the excavation of castle sites. Two important excavations were conducted in the late nineteenth century by Captain Morgan at Bishopston (Glamorgan) and General Pitt Rivers at Folkestone (Kent) (figure 5).

In 1912, two very important books appeared: Ella Armitage's *The Early Norman Castles of the British Isles* and A. Hamilton Thompson's *Military Architecture in England during the Middle Ages*. Both were crucial to the modern foundation of castle studies and still influence the way we think about the subject. Ella Armitage's emphasis on the novelty of Norman castle-building in the British Isles established a tradition that is still of influence. Its main modern protagonist was the late R. Allen Brown, whose books on English castles (1954 onwards) were widely read and respected, and who wrote the first Shire book on the

---

At the end of the long building enterprise at **Orford,** which had started in 1165, £58-2-8 was spent on a great ditch around the castle, with a surrounding palisade and bretasches, and a stone bridge across.

Et In Opat .ı. magni fossati circa Castellũ de Oreforḋ c̃
Heric̃ 7 Bretesc̃h 7 in Opat Pontis lapidei de eoḋ Castello .ʟvııı. ̃ıı. 7 .ıı. s̃. 7 .vııı. ḋ. p br̃ R̃ic de Luci . 7 p
visũ Rob de Valeiuis 7 .ıı. Normãnoȝ de Gipeswic̃h.

As part of on-going maintenance of the century-old castle at **Norwich,** £20-4-8 was spent on repairs to the stone bridge, palisade and three bretasches.

Et In Reparat̃ Pontis lapidei 7 Palicii . 7 .ııı. Bretesc̃har̃
in eoḋ castello de Norwic̃h .xx. l̃i. 7 .ıııı. s̃. 7 .vııı. ḋ. p br̃ . ℞ .
7 p visũ Phil†† de Hastiñg̃.

---

6. Extracts from the royal Pipe Roll of 1172–3, recording expenditure on building work at two royal castles in East Anglia: Orford and Norwich. English texts are authors' summaries. Latin texts are based on the edition published by the Pipe Roll Society.

subject (1985). Other important twentieth-century developments included the systematic compilation of county-based castle lists by the *Victoria County History* and the scientific recording of field monuments by the *Royal Commissions* in the United Kingdom and by the Archaeological Survey in Ireland. These sources form an invaluable resource for those researching castles (further reference to important publications and bodies will be found at the end of this book). Another outstanding contribution was the publication in 1963 of the medieval volumes of *The History of the King's Works*, a comprehensive compilation by H. M. Colvin and others of documentary data relating to the building, maintenance and administration of royal castles and other properties, based on Pipe Rolls and other sources (figure 6).

From the very beginnings, studies of castles have been necessarily interdisciplinary in scope, drawing on a number of diverse sources of data. Ella Armitage and her contemporaries advanced the subject on various fronts, for example by relating surviving physical sites to medieval documentary sources. As the twentieth century progressed, the repertoire of castellologists extended to include an even wider array of source material and methodologies, including, for instance, refined forms of archaeological excavation and ground survey, standing building analysis and aerial photography. In 1987, by the time the Castle Studies Group was founded, the need to study castles in a multifaceted but integrated way was well established and reflected directly in the wording of the group's foundation statement:

1: to promote the study of castles in all their forms and by all possible means: documentary studies, architectural history, fieldwork and excavation;

2: to promote the study of castles as resources for a more widely based appreciation of medieval society, emphasising their social and political history, their defensive and domestic evolution, their role in settlement development and their value as a source for the reconstruction of landscapes and economic environments.

A major theme of interest from the beginnings of modern castle studies has been the thorny problem of castle origins. In the late nineteenth century, Armitage and others emphasised the connection between castle-building and 'feudal' society in northern France. It was in this area that some of the earliest documentary references to castles occurred. From this evidence arose a theory of castle origins that depended on a 'diffusion' theme: castles and castle-building were seen to have been exported to other areas through conquest and colonisation. More recently, writers on the 'origins' issue have allowed for more flexible approaches to the subject. In a variety of countries, precursors to castles have been excavated, for example in England at Goltho (Lincolnshire) and Sulgrave (Northamptonshire), and in Ireland at Castleskreen (Co. Down), where Norman earth-and-timber castles overlay earlier high-status defended residences (figure 7). Archaeological study has also revealed how many castles, in many parts of Europe, were subject to physical evolution over

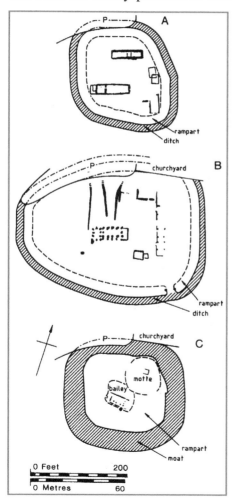

7. Goltho, Lincolnshire: the development of a pre-Conquest manorial site into a Norman castle, as reconstructed from excavated evidence. (Source: R. Morris, *Churches in the Landscape*, Dent, 1989)

8. Corfe Castle, Dorset. This aerial view highlights the elevated position of the royal stronghold, which controlled an important route to and from the Isle of Purbeck. Towards the top of the photograph can be identified the earthworks of a siege castle built on lower ground. (Crown copyright, NMR, English Heritage)

lengthy periods of time. The important site of Mirville (Normandy), for instance, was founded as an enclosed residence but only grew into a motte in around 1100. In a very real sense castles continued to 'originate' and evolve over long periods, so that a simple 'export' explanation is no longer satisfactory. Nevertheless, there is no doubt that situations of political and military necessity could give rise to the rapid expansion of castle-building. Classic examples of this process are the Norman Conquests of England, Wales, Scotland and Ireland, which saw an

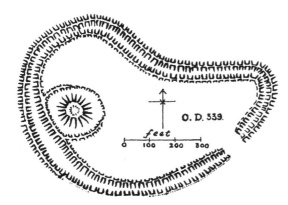

9. Hembury Castle, Buckfastleigh, Devon, as depicted in schematic fashion by A. H. Allcroft in *Earthwork of England*, 1908. This early work on English field monuments recognised the multi-phase character of many earthworks; here, a Norman motte has been inserted into the western end of a late prehistoric hillfort.

unprecedented boom in the construction of private defended residences as new lords consolidated their social and economic positions.

One profitable way of understanding castles is in a topographical sense, by examining their sites and their relationship with the human and physical landscape. It is a popular misconception that most castles were built on the tops of hills. While some sites in such positions did exist, are impressive and are usually of exceptionally high status (for

10. Cardiff Castle, Glamorgan, showing a Norman motte surmounted by a shell keep, with the restored defences of a Roman fort visible in the background. (Photograph: the authors)

example, Corfe, Dorset [figure 8]; Peveril, Derbyshire; and Beeston, Cheshire), far more common was the more modest rural castle built in a position essentially similar to that of any other medieval high-status residence. Particularly favoured positions were on valley sides and spur ends, which combined advantages of accessibility with visibility, drainage and, of course, defensibility. Although some castle-builders chose fresh sites for their fortifications, surprising numbers of castles were sited at points in the landscape whose significance had been recognised long before. The great Norman ringwork at Old Sarum was superimposed within an enclosure of Iron Age origin that was also occupied in the Anglo-Saxon period; other castles built within hillforts include Hembury (Devon) (figure 9) and the Herefordshire Beacon. Pevensey (East Sussex), Portchester (Hampshire) and Cardiff (Glamorgan) (figure 10) are among the many castles built within former Roman defences.

2
Castles: status and society

Who built castles, when and why? The answers to these apparently simple questions range across many centuries and many countries. In simple terms, castles were built by the richer and more powerful members of society. Although most castles were built for secular lords, a surprising number were the defended residences of ecclesiastical magnates, including prominent examples such as Old Sarum (Wiltshire), Rochester (Kent) and Sherborne (Dorset). But these groups contained many gradations of wealth and power and the social order was not static – in fact it was constantly changing as the fortunes of families rose and fell in the hierarchy. Notable was the tendency of incoming kings to reward their supporters, which might lead to castle-building. For example, Henry I's patronage of the de Redvers family led to the foundation or redevelopment of castles at Plympton (Devon) and Carisbrooke (Isle of Wight). The unfinished state of the fortified manor house at Kirby Muxloe (Leicestershire) is attributable to the summary execution by Richard III of its builder, William, Lord Hastings, barely three years after work had started.

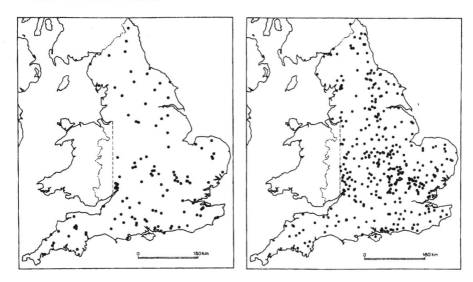

11. Distribution maps of different types of castle site in England, with the Welsh borderlands omitted. The map to the left shows ringworks (earthwork enclosures); that to the right shows the more plentiful mottes (artificial mounds). (Source: the authors)

Castle foundation was not evenly distributed in time or space. There was a great explosion of private fortification in the decades immediately following the Norman Conquest of England, which continued into the twelfth century. Comparable developments occurred, though not at the same time, in parts of Wales, Scotland and Ireland. Distributions are very uneven. Some areas, such as the border of England with Wales, contain remarkable densities of castles, reflecting the relative instability of this region as well as the popularity of castle-building among relatively minor members of the landholding classes. In England generally, distributions are influenced by tenurial and political as well as topographical factors (figure 11). The marked absence of castles in the hinterlands of medieval towns such as Bristol and London, for instance, is probably explained by policies of enforcement rather than any suggestion that the terrain was in some way unsuitable for castle-building. The fourteenth and fifteenth centuries saw quite different patterns of castle-building led by ambitious and newly successful members of the gentry class, building castles for the first time to make their mark on society and local landscapes. Good examples of castellated aristocratic residences in this mould include Nunney (Somerset, 1373) (figure 12)

12. Nunney Castle, Somerset: an unusual French-inspired tower house surrounded by a moat. (Photograph: the authors)

and Wardour (Wiltshire, 1393). These later castles, far from representing a 'decline', actually reflect the ongoing social importance of private fortification, even though they had reduced capacities for military involvement when compared with many of their predecessors. In conjunction, these processes led to the foundation of enormous numbers of castles, even in inland areas with relatively stable societies. In Bedfordshire, for example, no fewer than twenty-five castles of many descriptions were built, while Warwickshire contains thirty-one sites. An analogy is to be found at Coventry where, despite their distance from any border theatres of war, the burgesses spent much effort on building their own town walls from the fourteenth to the sixteenth century.

The reasons for castle-building and the purposes to which castles were put were similarly varied. These included serious military use (both offensive and defensive) but also commonly a variety of social and economic functions that are easily underestimated. The range of possible functions varied immensely from one place to another. At the simplest end of the scale, siege castles were essentially single-function sites, of specific purpose and short life. In the same category might be included watch-towers, such as Bledisloe (Gloucestershire), which was built on a high point at the edge of the Forest Dean. Other sites with a limited but important range of functions include those used as administrative centres related to the exploitation of valuable resources, such as Lydford (tin, in Devon) (figure 13) or Sauvey (in a royal forest,

13. Lydford Castle, Devon. This site was closely associated with the administration of the Devon Stannaries. The appearance of a keep constructed on the summit of a motte is an illusion; excavation has demonstrated the 'motte' to be a secondary, thirteenth-century feature, piled around the base of an existing tower, which was heightened at the same time. (Photograph: the authors)

Leicestershire). Many castles occupied by the tenants of great lords were simultaneously defended homes and manorial centres, built to oversee agricultural management át a local scale. The principal castles of secular barons and great ecclesiastical lords were, in contrast, the hubs of far more extensive networks of landed estates, which could extend across shires and even beyond. The impressive sites of Castle Acre (Norfolk), Conisbrough (South Yorkshire) and Sandal (West Yorkshire), for instance, were all castles and major estate centres of the de Warennes – one of the wealthiest and most powerful families in the Norman world, whose extensive holdings also reached across the English Channel.

Royal castles, in contrast, had a different balance of functions. Their political and military roles meant that their designs often represented the strongest and most impressive accomplishments of their age. They were often also among the biggest and most expensive castles, and they experienced lavish upgrading over many centuries. One of the clearest examples of this process is the major castle in London, commonly known, from its most famous structure, as the Tower of London (figure 14). Built initially as an embanked and ditched enclosure in the corner of the Roman city walls (*c*.1066–7), the great royal palace-fortress was developed through a series of additions and did not represent a single, unified design. Principal among these works were the construction of the White Tower later in the eleventh century, the enlargement of the fortress within a greatly extended walled enclosure by Henry III (1216–72) and the

14. The Tower of London, as depicted by W. Hollar in the seventeenth century. The view shows William I's White Tower, surrounded by later curtain walls and towers.

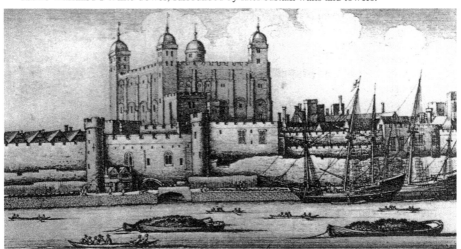

conversion of the site into a vast concentric castle through Edward I's addition of a further outer curtain wall (*c.*1275–85). Royal castles also had functions not found in other castles. They could act, for example, as treasuries, armouries, jails, palaces, the settings for state occasions and many other activities associated with kingship. Given the commonly itinerant royal lifestyle, such castles were only occasionally royal residences and their management was normally left in the hands of constables and other officials. Whereas a baronial castle lay at the heart of a complex social and economic network, royal castles tended to have only a relatively small associated estate though this commonly included access to a royal hunting resource.

Another reflection of the social significance of castle-builders lies in the juxtaposition of countless castles with parish churches, collegiate establishments, cathedrals and monasteries. All these institutions might at some stage benefit from the receipt of patronage from castle lords. Some parish churches even lay within castle baileys (for example, Laughton-en-le-Morthen, South Yorkshire, and Earl Shilton, Leicestershire). In addition, lords commonly built domestic chapels within their castles, and these were sometimes appropriated to a religious house elsewhere, of which the lord was patron. Paradoxically, however, in the Norman period it was not unknown for castle-building to disrupt churches and their graveyards, as at Barnstaple (Devon), Pontefract (West Yorkshire), Hereford, Worcester, and Malmesbury (Wiltshire).

Although castles were the product and symbol of a masculine military culture, this did not mean that women did not have an important role to play in day-to-day castle occupation. Women would have been immensely influential in the organisation of households, though gender-specific use is not readily apparent in surviving architectural evidence. Occasionally, the surviving relative of a deceased lord might continue as a powerful castle-holder in her own right, perhaps the most famous example being Isabella de Fortibus, Lady of the Isle of Wight and Carisbrooke Castle in the later thirteenth century. Sometimes, documentary evidence links women with particular parts of castles. For example, certain chambers might be apportioned in dower arrangements, while castle gardens could also be built for women. At Conwy, Edward I's queen was provided with a garden in a place of great political and military significance.

While each castle was the residence of a single individual and his or her immediate household, most were built to receive and sometimes accommodate an enormous range of other personnel from a variety of social backgrounds. Visitors of especially high status would bring their own retinues. These additional households might be accommodated in halls and chambers or, later, in high-status lodgings. The provision of

15. Bodiam Castle, East Sussex. The site is set within a large shallow lake, which, rather than having a principally defensive function, was probably designed to enhance the appearance of the castle. (Photograph: the authors)

the last is particularly well understood in castles of fourteenth-century date. At Castle Bolton (North Yorkshire), for instance, the Scropes' great late-fourteenth-century castle contained no fewer than eight identifiable suites for visiting households; a comparable site from southern Britain is Bodiam (East Sussex) (figure 15). Important baronial and royal castles could also accommodate men of knightly status owing 'castle guard' (a particular type of feudal tenure under which an individual would contribute to a castle's garrisoning in return for rights to land). The identities of men performing such duties are recorded in a remarkable fourteenth-century illustration of Richmond Castle (North Yorkshire) in the form of flags flying from different parts of the site's defences. The status of castles as estate centres meant that officials of various types would frequent them, while their economic roles would encourage the presence of craftspeople and traders from time to time. But not all the inhabitants of castles were human. Horses, in particular, were accommodated in many baileys or outer wards, either stabled or simply tethered. A sizeable stable block is recorded within the defences of Restormel Castle (Cornwall) in a survey of 1337, while environmental evidence recovered during excavation at Hen Domen (Powys) suggested the presence of animal fodder within the bailey.

Different social groups had different levels of access to the interiors of castles. Indeed, the organisation of 'social space' within surviving masonry buildings inside the defensive perimeters of castles has been the subject of many fascinating studies, showing how interiors were planned and access between different parts of the structure controlled. However, the surviving physical fabric of such buildings provides only a skeleton, the flesh of which must cautiously be reconstructed in other ways. In order to establish the functions of various rooms, secure identification of the meaning and relative status of interior features is essential. Fireplaces and garderobes, for instance, are useful indicators of regular domestic occupation, whereas the tracery of a window or the presence of a piscina would indicate a private chapel. In addition, we must bear in mind that our view of the interior of medieval buildings is an artificially bare one; in reality, living spaces were sometimes adorned with painted false ashlar, plasterwork, tapestries and other hangings, and forms of artificial lighting. In certain cases, it appears that the internal plans of donjons were conceived not to enhance defensibility but to provide magnificent domestic facilities that deliberately highlighted to visitors the status of their aristocratic occupants. For instance, any individual approaching the hall contained within the great twelfth-century donjon at Castle Rising (Norfolk) would first have to ascend an impressive stairway contained within a forebuilding before waiting in an unheated chamber set at a level slightly below the hall (figure 16). Having ascended the final short set of steps, the daytime visitor would doubtless be impressed by the way that the principal window within the hall cast light on the high table. Essentially similar methods of planning, designed to control access to lords in deliberate and sophisticated ways, are evident in the plans of donjons of different

16. Castle Rising, Norfolk: one of a number of donjons where research has emphasised the extent to which building designs were intended not only to protect, but also to impress. (Photograph: the authors)

dates, including those of Knaresborough (North Yorkshire) and Castle Hedingham (Essex). At the latter, architectural analysis has illuminated not only the high-status character of the donjon, but more specifically its association with the elevation of its owners, the de Veres, to the earldom of Oxford in 1141. The building was thus a specific statement intended to emphasise its family's social advancement.

If the very possession of a castle was a symbol of status, then the grant of royal permission to build one was a particularly jealously guarded right. 'Licences to crenellate' are known from the middle of the thirteenth century. In one sense, these represent the age-old authority of rulers over the building of private fortifications. Perhaps more significant, however, was the social significance of licences to crenellate as a measure of the status attached to the letter in which the act of commission was recorded. It is no coincidence that many licences to crenellate were granted to families whose wealth was a relatively recent acquisition and who were often first-time castle-builders. At Cooling Castle (Kent) part of the text of the royal permit granted to Sir John Cobham in 1381 was displayed in an inscription placed prominently on the impressive gatehouse (figure 17). Licences to crenellate must, however, be interpreted with caution. Not all late-medieval castle-building operations were accompanied by licences, while some town walls and ecclesiastical

17. The twin-towered gatehouse at Cooling, Kent, part of Sir John de Cobham's castle built in the 1380s. (Photograph: the authors)

precincts as well as secular castles were also the subject of licences. As in the Norman period, later episcopal palaces were often visually enhanced by architectural features borrowed from traditions of castle-building. An excellent example of this type of site is the palace of Acton Burnell (Shropshire), the subject of a licence granted to Bishop Robert Burnell in 1284.

The work of landscape archaeologists and garden historians has increasingly drawn attention to the fact that many castles were also components within wider landscapes designed for pleasure and entertainment. Although this seems rather at odds with traditional perceptions of castles as an essentially warlike phenomenon, it appears that the surroundings of many sites were purposefully designed to exhibit the residence and display its architectural qualities. Nowhere is this better represented than at Bodiam (East Sussex), where Sir Edward Dalyngrigge's magnificently preserved quadrangular castle, built in the

18. Leeds Castle, Kent. While the present appearance of this castle owes much to post-medieval rebuilding and landscaping, the site was founded in the eleventh century. (Crown copyright, NMR, English Heritage)

late 1380s, was surrounded by a fantastic waterscape that presented a shimmering vision, loaded with chivalric imagery, to anybody approaching the site. Another feature of this ornamental landscape was a viewing platform on the slopes above the castle that allowed the whole ensemble to be admired. Kenilworth Castle (Warwickshire) is another site surrounded by a shallow artificial lake that had aesthetic as well as defensive and other practical qualities (it also served as a fish pool). A later addition to the landscape around Kenilworth was the 'Pleasance in the Marsh' or moated banqueting house built on the edge of the mere by Henry V and designed to be accessible by boat. Other castles accompanied by ornamental lakes or ponds include Clun and Whittington (Shropshire), Leeds (Kent) (figure 18) and Ravensworth (North Yorkshire). Less dramatic were the small enclosed herb gardens that lay within or immediately beyond the baileys or outer wards of many castles. One of the best-surviving examples is the walled castle garden, probably dating to the thirteenth century, in the wild promontory castle of Tintagel (Cornwall), while at Stafford Castle a replica herb garden has been reconstructed. At some places, physical traces of garden features survive in the topography of the castles; at many more, documentary evidence of their maintenance reveals their former existence but no landscape evidence has survived.

3
Castles at war

From one perspective, the development of castles can be viewed as the product of an evolutionary struggle between increasingly sophisticated techniques of attack and progressively more scientific methods of defence (figure 19). This view of castle evolution is, however, rather simplistic. The defensive qualities of any castle were dependent not only upon its plan and construction but also on the strength and morale of its garrison and levels of provisioning. In addition, documentary accounts of sieges make it very clear that a castle could be prepared rapidly for war through the addition of features such as timber galleries to the tops of walls and

19. A medieval siege, as depicted by Viollet le Duc in the mid nineteenth century.

towers. But perhaps most importantly, we must remember that different castles were built to meet different levels of threat (from both their own societies and sometimes those beyond), and that not all were designed to withstand a full-scale siege. For instance, many of the numerous earth-and-timber castles on the Welsh Marches built by petty lords in the late eleventh and early twelfth centuries were intended as domestic defence and deterrence against small-scale raiding and even banditry rather than to meet organised invasion.

Castles dominated medieval warfare because they dominated the land, so that control of an area's castles was a prerequisite for effective authority over the territory. Alone, however, a castle was neither designed nor able to prevent the movement of hostile forces, and the border regions of Britain, as elsewhere, were characterised by high densities of sites rather than 'strings' of castles. The border county of Herefordshire, for instance, has an average density of one castle every 9 square kilometres.

It was not simply the need for defence against improving methods of attack that stimulated the escalation of castle-building between the eleventh and thirteenth centuries. Because castles were always symbols of their builders' power, the richest castle-builders in particular felt it necessary to demonstrate their wealth and status through the construction of the strongest castles that contemporary technology could provide. In this sense, castle-building was part of the 'arms race' that started in prehistory and is still with us today.

Defence was only one of a castle's roles in times of war. As some of the earliest castles raised by the Norman invaders in 1066 (for example Hastings, Sussex) demonstrate, the castle could also be an aggressive instrument of military conquest. In exposed regions the castle could occasionally act as a communal refuge, as at Bamburgh Castle (Northumberland) and, especially, in the Channel Islands, where the immense base-courts (or outer wards) of fortresses such as Grosnez (Jersey) frequently sheltered civilian populations. Other castles had military significance as arsenals. Important royal castles such as Nottingham, the Tower of London and Winchester were all repositories of siege machinery that could be rapidly deployed across the realm or, in the case of Portchester (Hampshire), for campaigns overseas. The royal stronghold of St Briavels (Gloucestershire) had particular importance as a centre for the administration of the iron industry in the Forest of Dean and as a store for crossbow bolts (quarrels). During the siege of Kenilworth (Warwickshire) in 1266, four thousand quarrels were ordered from St Briavels in June and a further six thousand in July.

Arrow loops became common features within castles from the late twelfth century (figures 20 and 21). These took a variety of forms,

20. An arrow loop at Warkworth Castle, Northumberland. Note the fishtail opening at the base, increasing visibility and the field of fire. (Photograph: the authors)

ranging from the simple vertical slit to those with a horizontal slit to give a cruciform appearance, and multiple offset horizontal slits are not unknown. A further variation was the use of oillets (openings at the ends of slits), to allow the bowman greater vision and manoeuvrability, but also giving a certain decorative effect to the exterior. All these features were splayed on the inside in order to widen the available field of fire. Detailed analysis of the disposition of arrow loops can illuminate how sophisticated techniques of defence could be. For instance, study of the provision of arrow loops at Framlingham (Suffolk) in the late twelfth century demonstrates that carefully placed multiple tiers of embrasures in the curtain wall, gatehouse and towers provided

21. Arrow loops piercing the merlons on the parapet of the early-fourteenth-century shell keep at Totnes Castle, Devon. (Photograph: the authors)

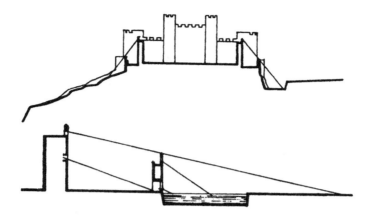

22. Sections through two of Edward I's late-thirteenth-century castles in North Wales, illustrating projected lines of archery fire from the battlements. The top diagram is of Harlech and the bottom of Beaumaris. (Source: Q. Hughes, 'Medieval firepower', *Fortress*, 8, 1991)

for both crossbow and longbow, offering interlocking fields of fire that covered weak points around the defences. This principle was further refined in the more symmetrical of Edward I's late-thirteenth-century castles in North Wales, such as Harlech (Gwynedd), where multilevel banks of arrow loops provided little or no dead ground between the concentric lines of defence and beyond (figure 22). But despite the application of such scientific techniques of defence, archers manning arrow loops were not invulnerable. Interesting experimental studies conducted at White Castle (Monmouthshire) have suggested that from a range of 25 yards (about 23 metres) beyond the defences an experienced archer was able to fire an arrow through a loop with a 30 per cent chance of success. It is, however, important to recognise that not all such features were necessarily purely military in function. Throughout much of the medieval period military architecture was also an expression of a chivalric culture, and sometimes outwardly military features were incorporated in castle designs for reasons of display.

In the eleventh and early twelfth centuries, methods of attacking castles were relatively simple. Graphic depictions of such warfare, including cavalry attack and setting fire to timber structures, occur in scenes from the Bayeux Tapestry. Chroniclers of this period also describe relatively unsophisticated assaults, although undermining and siege towers were occasionally employed. As the twelfth century progressed, siege warfare became more complex in style and scale, as did the responses made by castle defenders. Siege artillery – including the mangonel (a stone-throwing torsion-powered catapult), trebuchet (a stone-throwing counterweighted sling), and ballista or springald (similar to a crossbow,

23. A medieval trebuchet, as depicted by A. Hamilton Thompson in *Military Architecture in England during the Middle Ages,* 1912, reprinted 1975.

throwing a large bolt) – are a familiar part of many reconstructions of medieval sieges (figure 23). But we have remarkably little idea of precisely which types of artillery were deployed against castles during sieges, as chroniclers almost invariably refer to such engines with the Latin word *petraria.* It was not unknown for siege machines to be used in a defensive capacity by castle garrisons: at the siege of Kenilworth (Warwickshire) in 1266, for instance, stone-throwing engines were used to counter those employed by the attacking royal forces.

Archaeological or other physical evidence of the direct effects of siege warfare on castles can be elusive. A famous example of a castle partially rebuilt following a successful siege is Rochester (Kent). The south-east corner turret of the great tower is cylindrical, unlike the other three turrets, which are rectangular, because it was rebuilt during the 1220s, following the collapse of this part of the structure after undermining by the forces of King John during a famous siege in 1215 (figure 24). The rebuilding of Rochester was also extended to the curtain wall, where the corner nearest the damaged part of the great tower

24. Rochester Castle, Kent, showing the single round tower built on the corner of the siege-damaged donjon and the rounded bastion added to the adjacent corner of the curtain wall. (Photograph: the authors)

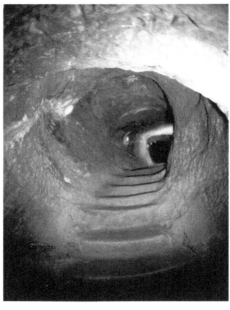

25. A medieval mine under St Andrews Castle, Fife. (Crown Copyright ©; reproduced courtesy of Historic Scotland)

was modified to incorporate a formidable archery battery, concentric in shape with the tower's reconstructed corner. Another war-damaged castle is the border fortress of Dolforwyn (Powys), where repair of the curtain wall in the aftermath of an English siege of 1277 can be identified by the use of a distinctive mortar and building stone. Excavations at the site have remarkably recovered a number of catapult balls shaped from volcanic rock and sandstone, including some recovered at the original point of impact and others incorporated into later walls and cobbled floors. Beneath the castle at St Andrews (Fife) are preserved a remarkable mine and countermine, both dug during the siege of 1546–7 (figure 25), while among the labyrinthine tunnels beneath Dover Castle (Kent) is a series of countermining galleries probably related to the siege of 1216.

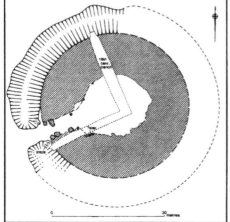

The most tangible physical evidence of medieval sieges is the remains of temporary fortifications sometimes erected in military opposition to castles. Although many of these works are documented, comparatively few survive and only one

26. A plan of a medieval siege castle at Exeter, Devon, probably built under the orders of King Stephen during his siege of the city in 1136. The site, known as Danes Castle, was fully excavated in 1993 during the redevelopment of the reservoir beneath which it had been buried since the mid nineteenth century. (Source: Exeter Archaeology)

(Danes Castle, Exeter, Devon) has been excavated in detail (figure 26). Examples mentioned in documentary sources but now entirely vanished include Bamburgh (Northumberland), Dunster (Somerset) and Downton (Wiltshire). Those siege castles that do survive form two distinct types. First are those fortifications erected within the immediate vicinity of another castle (although usually beyond crossbow range), forming a platform for direct bombardment or armed assault. An excellent example is the site known as 'The Rings', a small ringwork and bailey merely 300 metres distant from Corfe Castle (Dorset), against which it was raised by King Stephen in 1139 (figure 8). The second category comprises 'counter castles', which were built at greater distance from their prey in order to blockade it. An earthwork in north Wiltshire known as 'Cams Hill' appears to have been such a parasitic castle. It was built in 1144 by Robert, Earl of Gloucester, against Malmesbury, overlooking a crossing of the River Avon about 1.5 km south of the town. We can, however, question whether short-term fortifications such as these were, in reality, castles, as they will have lacked the residential qualities that were essential to the medieval castle. In a different category altogether are the unusual remains of earthen platforms for siege engines around Berkhamsted (Hertfordshire). At least seven such features lie in an arc around the motte and seem likely to have supported the trebuchets deployed against the castle by Prince Louis in 1216. Notably, while the trebuchet was not introduced until the thirteenth century, the other principal stone- or bolt-throwing engines all ultimately had Roman or earlier ancestry, as did many other methodologies of siege warfare.

It is important not to oversimplify the relationship between the development of gunpowder artillery and the evolution of castles. The introduction of this technology did not result in an overnight change in techniques of fortification, nor did it alone cause the 'decline' of the castle, which was a far more complex process. After firearms were first represented in English manuscripts, in 1326–7, their impact on castle architecture was significant but not revolutionary. Indeed, the earliest documented gunports in Britain were incorporated within the wall of a monastic precinct (Quarr Abbey, Isle of Wight, *c*.1365), while the first specialised gun-tower (Cow Tower, Norwich, *c*.1398) contributed to the defence of the town rather than forming part of a castle. From the second half of the fourteenth century, however, simple gunports were incorporated into extant castles (as at Carisbrooke, Isle of Wight) or built in new ones (as at Cooling, Kent). Good examples of gunports from the fifteenth century can be found at Berry Pomeroy (Devon) (figure 27), Raglan (Monmouthshire) and Kirby Muxloe (Leicestershire). These features generally took the form of an inverted keyhole, comprising a circular embrasure for the firearm accompanied by a vertical

27. A late-fifteenth-century gunport in Margaret's Tower, Berry Pomeroy Castle, Devon. Unique in England, the design incorporates two openings (oillets), splayed both on the inside and outside, for handguns or observation, and a separate rectangular cannon port (visible at the bottom of the photograph). (Photograph: the authors)

observation slot, although variations are known. They were designed for handguns or small artillery pieces and for close-in defence; more importantly, these gunports were incorporated into traditional castle designs not otherwise intended to accommodate or resist artillery. The new technology did not, therefore, produce a new 'type' of castle. We should also not overlook the prestige that accrued to the owners of castles equipped with gunports, and it is significant that they were also incorporated in town gates and towers (for example God's House Tower, Southampton, c.1417), where they were clearly emblems of status as well as military features.

Dartmouth Castle (Devon) was an especially innovative structure, built from 1481 by the townsfolk, with royal sponsorship, to protect their vulnerable anchorage (figure 28). A fascinating blend of old and

new design, the structure features novel gunports, comprising large square embrasures with correspondingly broad fields of fire. But also, in terms of its elevated tower-like appearance, it harks back to the symbolism of the donjon. It was not until the co-ordinated programme of coastal defence initiated by Henry VIII, however, that the need to accommodate and defend against artillery came to dominate the designs of fortifications, as exemplified by sites such as Deal (Kent) and St Mawes (Cornwall), which were staffed by professional gunners.

28. Dartmouth Castle, Devon, showing the site's position overlooking the mouth of the Dart estuary. (Photograph: the authors)

4
The contribution of archaeology

Much of the evidence discussed in this book is visible above ground, especially in the form of upstanding masonry remains and surviving earthworks. These represent, however, but one dimension of the total remains of medieval castles. Equally important are the buried remains, including structures as well as artefactual and environmental evidence, which can illuminate many aspects of daily life in and around these sites. While buried remains are generally the domain of the archaeologist and upstanding remains the concern of the architectural historian, it is important to remember that this distinction is largely artificial: all types of evidence are parts of an integrated body of data and complement one another (figure 29).

Modern archaeological study of medieval castles comprises far more than the exposure of lost structures. Buried deposits in castles commonly also include a wealth of evidence that sheds light on the social and economic lives of their occupants, and the interrelationship between sites and their environments. Categories of data commonly encountered

29. Open-area excavation within the bailey of Launceston Castle, Cornwall. Large-scale excavation of the site over many years produced data that complemented the evidence provided by the standing masonry structures, some of which are visible. (Photograph: the authors)

include pottery, metalwork and palaeoenvironmental evidence such as animal bones, pollen, seeds, beetles and molluscs. The excavation of a buried drain at Barnard Castle (Durham), for instance, has provided an invaluable snapshot of aristocratic diet in the fifteenth century. The remains of a medieval feast showed the consumption of local products, including meat, poultry and freshwater fish, as well as the exploitation of resources drawn from further afield, including oysters and saltwater fish. As archaeological sites, castles certainly provide a wide array of contexts favouring the accumulation and preservation of such data, in particular where ditches, drains, moats and cisterns contain waterlogged deposits. The study of the animal bone assemblage at Okehampton (Devon) provided a remarkable insight into the environment surrounding this site and, in particular, the management of adjacent moorland for the intensive exploitation of deer, revealing replacement of red deer with greater numbers of fallow deer in the early fourteenth century (figure 30). An excellent example of pottery study from a castle is Sandal (West Yorkshire). The range of ceramic products at this site reflects enduring short- and long-distance contacts between the castle and other estates held by its lords (the de Warenne Earls of Surrey) in Yorkshire and south-east England. Twelfth-century metalwork assemblages from a number of excavated sites demonstrate the variety of everyday objects to whose purchase castle communities had access. Interesting similarities in élite material culture may be observed at, for instance, sites as far apart as Castle Acre (Norfolk), Laugharne (Carmarthenshire) and Hen Domen (Powys) (figure 31).

There was no such thing as an earthwork castle. There is, however, an enormous range and quantity of castle earthworks. These represent a

30. Excavated deer antlers *in situ* in the bailey at Okehampton Castle, Devon. (Photograph: the authors)

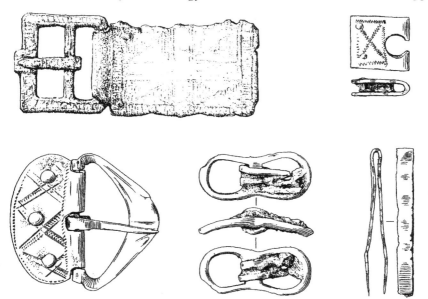

31. Twelfth-century copper-alloy objects excavated from Hen Domen Castle, Powys, including buckles and tweezers. (Source: the authors)

medieval application of an enduring tradition of building stretching from prehistory to the post-medieval era. Principal among surviving earthworks are those defensive structures including mounds and ramparts that were built from the upcast of ditches, although it was not unknown for the sites of castles to be carved from bedrock, as at Goodrich (Herefordshire) and Mountsorrel (Leicestershire). Beyond the defences of many castles lie less prominent but equally important earthworks of non-defensive character, including the sites of deserted settlements, fishponds, garden features, field systems and hollow-ways. Although many of these minor earthworks have been destroyed or disrupted, major ones have remained surprisingly resilient and are still prominent features of our landscapes and townscapes.

In castle studies, three words are commonly encountered in descriptions of major earthworks: 'motte', 'ringwork' and 'bailey'. But while the words 'motte' and 'bailey' derive ultimately from medieval terminology, the term 'ringwork' is a form of modern archaeological jargon. Mottes were artificial mounds of earth or broken rock, providing elevated positions for defensive or other high-status structures, usually initially of timber but occasionally of stone. These features could vary from

32. A Norman motte at Thetford Castle, Norfolk. One of the largest mottes ever constructed in Britain, this feature was built in the corner of a Saxon settlement in the late eleventh century. (Copyright: Norfolk Archaeology and Museums Service)

immense creations such as the motte at Thetford (Norfolk) (figure 32), with a base diameter of almost 100 metres and a height of 20 metres, to other examples only a couple of metres in elevation. Although some mottes were raised on greenfield sites (for example Sandal, West Yorkshire, which was built over a medieval field system), some were created by remodelling relict landscape features such as barrows (for example Driffield, East Yorkshire). Mottes are commonly regarded as an early feature of castle design that not only gave an elevated physical position but also expressed the power and authority of their builders. For this reason, mottes were frequently reused in the later medieval rebuilding of castles as they continued to provide prominent visible building platforms with resonances of status. The Percy family's remarkable late-fourteenth-century donjon at Warkworth (Northumberland), for instance, perpetuated the site of a motte that was already centuries old, as did the Earl of Cornwall's thirteenth-century donjon at Launceston (Cornwall) (figure 33). Those mottes without evidence of surmounting masonry structures sometimes have flat summits, although a surprising number have concave tops, suggesting

33. An eleventh-century motte with twelfth- and thirteenth-century stone structures at Launceston Castle, Cornwall. (Photograph: the authors)

the earlier presence of stone or timber structures formerly enveloped by the earthwork.

Ringworks were ditched and embanked enclosures usually characterised by defences that were massive in relation to their area. While the great enclosure castle built in Exeter (Devon) by William the Conqueror in 1068 occupied the northern corner of the city, another ringwork erected as a siege castle outside the city in 1136 by King Stephen, in opposition to the royal castle, was tiny in comparison, having a circular internal area only 18 metres across (figure 26). Among the most impressive ringworks in Britain is Castle Rising (Norfolk). The massive earthwork defences of this site, enclosing an oval area and partly burying an earlier church, were remodelled in the late twelfth or early thirteenth century so that the rampart stood 10 metres above the natural ground surface, topped by a timber palisade. While the reasons why a lord might choose to construct a ringwork as opposed to a motte remain rather obscure, the fact that modestly sized ringworks could be built comparatively rapidly was probably an important factor, and regional fashion may have been another.

Baileys were enclosed courtyards appended to a principal defensive unit such as a motte, ringwork or donjon. They could exist either singly or as multiple units, and could again take a variety of shapes and sizes.

Windsor Castle (Berkshire) originated as a central motte flanked by two baileys – a plan that remains evident despite the site's continuous occupation and remodelling to the present day. Very exceptionally, two mottes could be found attached to the same bailey enclosure, as at Lewes (East Sussex) and Lincoln. The earthworks at many castle baileys show the possible sites of perimeter towers, now represented by bulbous features at entrances or other critical points of the circuit. In addition, bailey interiors sometimes contain the vestiges of building platforms or grassed-over foundations, visible as humps and bumps. While the earthworks of numerous castles are major landscape features that have withstood the ravages of time, in some cases they have been drastically reduced or even totally removed. A small motte and bailey at Acton Bank, Lydbury North (Shropshire), is visible only from the air as a crop-mark; other mottes now stand as isolated features whose bailey enclosures have been ploughed out, as at Beaumont Chase (Rutland).

While mottes, ringworks and baileys have been described as distinct categories of earthwork, there is excavated evidence that one type could, on occasion, be converted into another. At Goltho (Lincolnshire), for instance, a ringwork was converted into a tiny motte and bailey through the imposition of a motte on its perimeter (figure 7), whereas at

34. The north tower and hall of Stokesay Castle, Shropshire, showing the skeleton of a timber-framed jettied upper chamber of the late thirteenth century with later alterations. (Photograph: the authors)

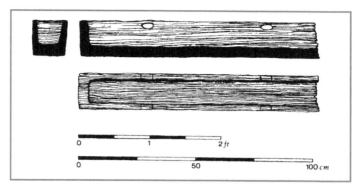

35. Preserved oak timber from the waterlogged bailey ditch at Hen Domen Castle, Powys, representing part of the palisade foundation from the crest of the rampart above. This slotted base-plate would have held substantial upright timbers. (Source: the authors)

Aldingham (Cumbria) a ringwork was filled in to create a motte. This can make the interpretation of castle evolution on the basis of earthwork evidence alone extremely hazardous. Only extensive excavation can reveal the chronological development of these sites.

No timber castle remains above ground, although in several places masonry structures incorporate timber components, as at Stokesay (Shropshire) (figure 34). Indeed, we must be careful not to draw a misleadingly simple distinction between 'timber' and 'stone' castles; many sites employed mixed building technologies both in their defences and in their domestic structures. In addition, documentary and pictorial evidence reminds us that domestic buildings might be of timber though enclosed by stone defences, or vice versa.

Overwhelmingly, however, it is only through painstaking excavation that the structural and other evidence of timber castles can be revealed. To date, only a tiny fraction of the total number of timber sites has been excavated, and the majority of these explorations have been small in scale. Such sites offer a particular challenge to the excavator for three reasons. First, only in waterlogged conditions will physical remains of buried timbers survive (figure 35), so the evidence normally encountered is the negative or 'ghost' traces left by rotted timbers in post-holes and other features. Second, there was a strong tradition of timber-framing in medieval building, also known to have been employed extensively in castle-building. Resulting structures, massive though they may have been, do not necessarily leave recoverable evidence proportionate to the scale and significance of the buildings themselves. Third, like most occupation sites, timber castles were rarely of one phase. Either through episodes of rebuilding or through processes after abandonment, much

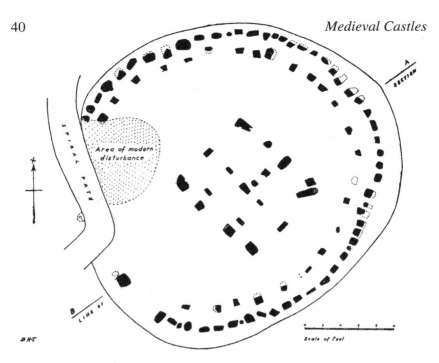

36. A plan of excavated features on the summit of the motte at Abinger, Surrey. One of the first excavations to reveal the remains of motte-top structures, the work at Abinger has been immensely influential. Nevertheless, reconstruction of superstructures from foundation evidence is notoriously difficult, and the customary interpretation of this ground plan as evidence of a stilted watch-tower is open to debate. (Source: B. Hope-Taylor, 'The excavation of a motte at Abinger, Surrey', *Archaeological Journal*, 107, 1950)

original evidence will have been obscured or be unrecoverable.

A castle excavation important in the development of medieval archaeology was carried out *c*.1950 at Abinger (Surrey). Here, the motte top revealed a collection of post-holes representing a circular palisade enclosing a tower, thought by the excavator to have stood on stilts, resembling a watch-tower rather than a residential donjon (figure 36). Other excavated sites with quite different structures include the motte at South Mimms (Hertfordshire), where a timber tower was partly contained within the mound, and Lismahon (Co. Down), where the motte carried a small hall flanked by a stilted timber tower. A sharply contrasting example is Castle Tower, Penmaen (West Glamorgan). With an internal area of only about 30 by 20 metres, this little coastal ringwork contained a hall to one side of the enclosure, the single entrance to which was protected by a simple two-storey gatehouse. This fortification was the seat of a petty lord commanding many fewer resources than a powerful Norman magnate.

37. An aerial view of the earthworks of the timber (motte and bailey) castle at Hen Domen, Powys. (Source: Clwyd-Powys Archaeological Trust)

38. The structures of the motte and bailey at Hen Domen Castle underwent a continuous process of redevelopment from the late eleventh to the late thirteenth century. This illustration, by Peter Scholefield, is an artist's reconstruction of the northern half of the bailey as it may have appeared around the middle of the twelfth century. Note the crowded nature of the bailey and its profusion of domestic and defensive structures.

By far the most extensively excavated and best-understood timber castle in Britain is the motte and bailey of Hen Domen (Powys), the precursor of Montgomery Castle (figure 37). This site was founded in the late eleventh century by Roger de Montgomery, Earl of Shrewsbury. His castle was massively defended and provided with large and simple domestic buildings. In the twelfth century the castle became the *caput* (or head) of a small marcher lordship and was rebuilt to provide a more varied array of domestic structures for a Flemish family, the de Boulers, that was now more normally resident. The motte carried a timber version of a donjon, while the bailey contained upper and lower halls, a chapel, a granary and many other lesser structures (figure 38). In the thirteenth century, when King Henry III built a new castle at Montgomery, Hen Domen was redesigned as a subsidiary site with fewer buildings.

These and other excavations show that the structural reality of timber castles was always far more complex than the surface remains of their earthworks superficially suggest. The pattern of evidence recovered in the excavations of timber castles reveals that these sites were as varied and individualistic in their appearance, and often no less imposing, than their counterparts built in stone. While some timber castles were subsequently rebuilt in stone, many were not and were refurbished using timber. Thus timber castles were not simply a plentiful feature of

39. A view of excavated masonry structures, including a barbican and donjon, on and around the motte of Sandal Castle, West Yorkshire. (Photograph: the authors)

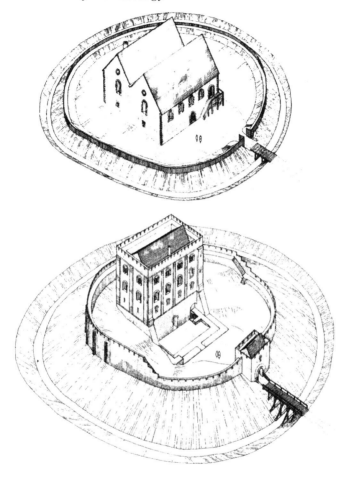

40. A reconstruction of the early and later phases of Castle Acre, Norfolk, based on the results of excavations on the upper part of the site. (Source: J. G. Coad and A. D. F. Streetham, 'Excavations at Castle Acre Castle, Norfolk, 1972–77', *Archaeological Journal*, 139, 1982)

the medieval landscape but one of equal social importance to the more obvious stone-built castles whose remains still survive above ground. Their impressiveness is also sometimes suggested by contemporary pictorial evidence as well as by written descriptions.

Archaeology has also added substantially to our understanding of stone castles. Far more than simply clearing stone structures of rubble, excavation at a number of sites has indicated the surviving detail of masonry remains and has invariably cast light on the structural development of buildings. Dolforwyn (Powys) is perhaps the best-known example of a large-scale excavation at the end of the twentieth century and has revolutionised our understanding of a castle otherwise lost to view; operations of similar scale have taken place at sites such as Bolingbroke (Lincolnshire) and Sandal (West Yorkshire) (figure 39). At Launceston (Cornwall), excavation has exposed a fascinating sequence of developments, including the replacement of timber bailey defences with stone, and recovered the plan of a suite of thirteenth-century domestic structures within the enormous bailey. Excavation at Edlingham Castle (Northumberland) has indicated a very different sequence. Here, because of unstable political circumstances and seigneurial ambition, a small, undefended stone-built hall-house was converted into a castle *c*.1340. The site was transformed by the addition of a tower, curtain wall and gatetower with drawbridge and portcullis at a time when traditions of private defence in central England were to some extent in decline.

The excavation of stone castles can produce results equally startling as those relating to earth-and-timber fortifications, no more so than at Castle Acre (Norfolk) (figure 40). Here, extensive excavation on the upper part of the site showed a sequence of events that is unlike that at any other known site and indeed challenges many of our traditional preconceptions of castle origins and evolution. The earliest Norman structure resembled a stone-built country house enclosed by a modest bank and palisade, rather than a strong fortification. In two stages, however, culminating in the 1150s, the site was transformed, first by a radical strengthening of its surrounding defences, and then by the conversion of the domestic building into a donjon. The site has a large bailey containing the grassed-over foundations of other domestic buildings, reminding us that, fascinating though this sequence is, it represents only part of the potential of a far more extensive archaeological resource.

5
The contribution of architectural studies

The preceding chapter illustrated how much of the evidence for castles has disappeared and is amenable to recovery only through excavation. It is tempting, but erroneous, to assume that because some castles have substantial stone buildings surviving above ground, they are fully comprehensible, their buildings providing a full guide to their appearance when occupied. In fact, stone structures pose considerable challenges of interpretation, and only by employing a wide range of analytical techniques can the messages that they contain be understood. Such structures can include defensive buildings, such as gatehouses, towers and curtain walls. They can also include residential or domestic buildings, including halls, chambers, kitchens, chapels, and other structures that might combine various functions, such as great towers or donjons and large gatehouses (figures 41 and 42). Additional evidence available for architectural study includes those features relating to construction (for example, masonry styles, putlog holes for scaffolding and masons' marks) and others relating to adornment or functional use (such as

41. The fourteenth-century gatehouse of Dunstanburgh Castle, Northumberland. This type of twin-towered design was widely used from the thirteenth century onwards, retaining some of the symbolism of the great tower or donjon. (Photograph: the authors)

42. An architectural detail of the interior of the circular nave of a Norman chapel within Ludlow Castle, Shropshire. The round-headed arches forming the blind arcade show alternate chevron and wave mouldings. (Photograph: the authors)

43. Herstmonceux Castle, East Sussex. While the highly decorative brick-built front dates from the mid fifteenth century, much of the remainder of the castle was demolished during rebuilding in 1777. (Photograph: the authors)

44. The gatehouse of Exeter Castle, Devon, dating from the castle's foundation in 1068 and displaying a remarkable combination of Norman and Anglo-Saxon architectural features. The entrance arch was later blocked and a new entrance to the site made to one side. (Photograph: the authors)

machicolation, crenellation, murder holes, portcullis slots and bridge abutments, arrow loops and gunports).

Earlier writers on medieval castles often used the phrase 'military architecture'. This phrase has to some extent fallen out of favour, as commentators have emphasised the residential qualities of castles and the social, even symbolic, attributes of their buildings. In fact, the phrase 'military architecture' deserves better, if more refined, use. Castles, in common with fortified sites of many other periods, displayed features that went far beyond the needs of simple utilitarian defence. It is this attention to non-functional detail – often conceived and realised with aesthetic qualities as well as a high level of technical expertise – that makes the word 'architecture' appropriate in the military context. The brick-built front of Herstmonceux, East Sussex (*c*.1440), for instance, is far more a showpiece of architectural sophistication than a defensive structure (figure 43). This phenomenon was not, however, restricted to the later Middle Ages. There are indications that ostentation was a consistent theme throughout castle development but was more apparent in some contexts than others. Some of the earliest stone-built gatehouses, such as Exeter (Devon) (figure 44) and Ludlow (Shropshire), had gallery-type features at first-floor level that had little utilitarian function and can most appropriately be understood as display features, as can the impressive Romanesque detail on the exteriors of Norman keeps such as Castle Rising (Norfolk).

Comparisons with non-defended buildings are relevant. A great country house will almost certainly be considered a piece of 'architecture' whereas a simple vernacular farmhouse may be better described as a 'building'. It is interesting to speculate whether, in the complex hierarchy of castle design, there was a point below which the word 'building' would be more appropriate and above which 'architecture' would apply. It is likely, for example, that temporary siege castles, or minor motte structures, or the smallest sorts of late-medieval northern border 'pele' or tower house, would be devoid of any elaboration deserving the title 'architecture'. At the other end of the spectrum, however, the donjon at Rochester (Kent) contains fine internal Romanesque detail, which compares with any contemporary major ecclesiastical building. At Norwich, the castle donjon, with its fine blind arcading, displays clear links with the Norman architecture of the nearby cathedral. Such considerations were not confined to stone building. In the twelfth century, the timber donjon on the bishop's motte at Durham, described by a contemporary writer, was a fittingly ornate counterpart for the adjacent cathedral. While it has been common to separate study of medieval castles from that of post-medieval country mansions, increasingly acknowledged is the role of the castle, amongst its many functions, as a high-status gentry house. Thus there is some continuity between the medieval and later centuries, across which the notion of 'polite architecture' had a long evolution.

Time and again, experience has shown that the fullest understanding of castle buildings emerges from their thorough recording on paper, in

45. An architectural drawing of the remains of the twelfth-century donjon at Plympton, Devon. This isometric projection is based on a detailed structural survey of the fragmentary remains of this shell keep, whose stone fabric was internally reinforced with timber. (Source: the authors)

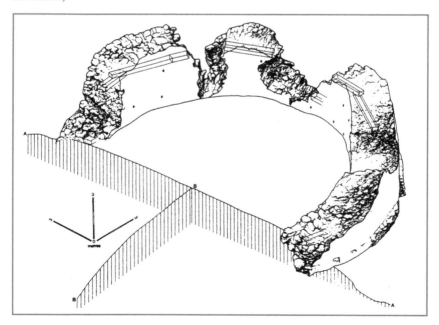

photograph and (increasingly) in digitised, computer-stored record. It is important to appreciate all perspectives of a building – in plan, in elevation and in individual details – but also to recognise that these are complementary parts of a whole (figure 45). As emphasised above, this whole may also include elements that lie below ground and from which the upstanding building cannot sensibly be divided. Parts of a building may now be completely absent, ranging from minor sections of masonry to whole components of the structure. However, careful recording of what does remain can lead to reliable reconstruction of that which has disappeared. Levels of recording vary according to circumstances. Sometimes it is appropriate to record every stone in a wall, whether drawn by hand or from images generated by photographic techniques. In other circumstances, less detail is recorded, for example when a wall is composed wholly of rough rubble construction. High-quality conservation also benefits from being carried out in partnership with detailed building analysis, as for instance at Okehampton (Devon) from the 1970s onwards. Such data have many values. They can lead to informative reconstruction drawings and can assist in the interpretation of building function, evolution and construction techniques.

It is automatic, indeed almost mandatory, in archaeological thinking to assemble data into chronological and spatial patterns and to identify recurrent 'types' of site or artefact. In castle studies, this process has led to the popularisation of such categories of masonry structure as 'palace keep', 'tower keep', 'circular/polygonal keep', 'concentric castle', 'quadrangular castle' and so on. These are useful as long as it is remembered that they are nothing more than broad generalisations. The most famous group of castles in Britain, those built by Edward I in North Wales, is a case in point (figure 46). All these sites – Flint and Rhuddlan (started 1277); Harlech, Conwy and Caernarfon (started 1283); and Beaumaris (started 1295) – were built for the same king to fulfil a common strategic goal but are quite different from one another in plan and do not show a simple evolutionary sequence. Despite the crucial role played by the mason Master James of St George at most of these castles, their plans reveal a blend of old and new ideas and sometimes adaptation to older sites and their topographies. Only two of these sites (Harlech and Beaumaris) were truly planned in the 'concentric' fashion – a label now frequently associated with this period of castle-building.

A traditional approach to the interpretation of castle architecture is to create a general sequence of evolution whereby sites grew in military sophistication until *c.*1300, after which there was progressively greater emphasis on domestic planning, comfort and appearance. This appealing narrative approach has been immensely influential in the modern study of castles. Increasingly, however, commentators have acknowledged

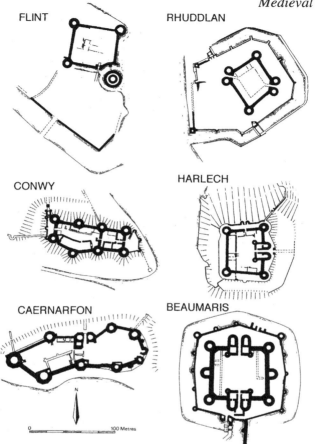

46. Plans of Edward I's principal castles in North Wales. (Source: C. Platt, *The Castle in Medieval England and Wales*, 1982)

the great individuality with which castle-building enterprises were approached. Castles were essentially built for individuals, whose preferences, resources and requirements differed enormously. This underlines the fact that, whatever their defensible qualities, most castles were essentially homes to be lived in (figure 47). In the eleventh and twelfth centuries, although castles undoubtedly could be very defensive, their domestic accommodation often reflected the highest available standards of their day. In the fourteenth and fifteenth centuries, the improvements in the planning and standard of domestic accommodation that we find in castles reflects not a change in attitude peculiar to castle-

47. An early-thirteenth-century fireplace in the top floor of the donjon of Odiham, Hampshire. (Photograph: the authors)

builders but a raised expectation more widely apparent throughout society. Thus, just as improved standards were to be found in rural and urban buildings, hospitals and collegiate buildings and in monasteries, so also improved standards are to be found within castles. It was not only castles that were changing in later centuries, therefore, but the wider world of domestic architecture.

In understanding castle evolution, informative parallels may also be drawn with ecclesiastical architecture. Here, we may define a broad evolutionary sequence of styles, through various phases of Romanesque and Gothic. But what is most striking is the individualistic achievements of the great cathedral- and abbey-building operations that moved these styles forward. Within the wide range of castle-building there similarly exists a degree of individuality, from minor variations on traditional themes to extremely idiosyncratic designs promoted by rich patrons and their builders. Although the architectural individuality of stone castles is still apparent, the presumed individuality of timber castles is hidden from us by the lack of structural evidence surviving above ground.

48. Chepstow Castle, Monmouthshire, showing the interior of the donjon. The lower level retains the Romanesque style of the original late-eleventh-century building; above this the thirteenth-century rebuilding was in a later, Gothic style. (Photograph: the authors)

We must also remember that, in broader terms, the designs of castles underwent an evolution from predominantly Romanesque to Gothic styles either side of *c.*1200, although many surviving sites, like churches, incorporate elements of both styles (figure 48). Indeed, very few sites display only one phase of development, the majority showing contributions from many generations over several centuries. It follows that, just as is the case in modern built environments, medieval castle sites (and church sites) would have been subject to building operations throughout a considerable proportion of their lifetimes. This contrasts with the tendency sometimes displayed by archaeologists to assume that evidence in the field represents rationally thought-out castle-building projects brought swiftly to perfect fruition. In reality, the medieval landscape is likely to have had its share of incomplete enterprises, projects that took a long time to complete and others doomed to failure. Surprising though it may seem, the inordinately expensive site of Beaumaris (Anglesey) – the last and most sophisticated of Edward I's castles in North Wales – was never completed. The much earlier and simpler site of Burwell (Cambridgeshire) is another that was left incomplete, as indicated by its surviving spoilheaps, now visible as grassed-over earthworks. Another caveat of the 'typological evolution' approach to castle study is that it is led by consideration of the innovative – castle-building operations at the 'sharp end' of contemporary architectural thought and experimentation, such as William the Conqueror's palace keep at Colchester (Essex) and Hamelin, Earl Warenne's circular keep at Conisbrough (South Yorkshire) (*c.*1180). However, to a contemporary traveller viewing the built environment of medieval Britain, more striking would have been the mixture of old and new castle sites, at various stages of development or decline and displaying varying degrees of sophistication. In this quantitative sense, perhaps the 'blunt end' of castle-building operations would have been more obvious and important than the 'sharp end'.

Equally, it is a mistake to try to fit all castles into a rigid sequence of evolutionary development. Many were individualistic in design to the point of being unique. A splendid example, reassessed around 1990, is the donjon at Orford started by Henry II in 1165 near the Suffolk coast (figure 49). Quite unlike any other building elsewhere in Britain, this royal castle does not easily fit into any categorisation and was traditionally labelled as representing a transitional phase in the evolution of the keep from rectangular to circular designs. More recent analysis has revealed far greater architectural complexity in the design, survey and construction of this building than was previously recognised – drawn heavily from traditions far beyond Britain. Its real importance lay in its statement of architectural innovation as an emblem of royal authority in its region.

Although castles do not show nearly as much regional variation as, for instance, parish churches and vernacular buildings, it is easy to overlook the fact that certain regional qualities can be observed in castle design. This can be detected in two forms. First, the details of a castle might mirror those of a nearby major ecclesiastical building, as at the cathedrals and castles in Lincoln and Norwich. Second, the role of local building and crafts industries, together with limitations or possibilities posed by the availability of local materials, might sometimes exert a profound influence on the castles of a particular region. For example, south-west England and South Wales displayed a marked favouritism between the twelfth and thirteenth centuries for circular shell keeps and tower keeps, including prominent examples at Launceston, Restormel and Trematon (Cornwall), Barnstaple, Plympton and Totnes (Devon), Pembroke (Pembrokeshire), Tretower (Powys) and Skenfrith (Monmouthshire). In this and in other ways, the Bristol

49. Orford Castle, Suffolk, showing the standing remains of the unusual late-twelfth-century donjon, surrounded by the grassed-over earthworks of further masonry structures lost to view. (Crown copyright, NMR, English Heritage)

50. Tattershall Castle, Lincolnshire. This magnificent brick-built tower was constructed *c.*1434–5 for Ralph, Lord Cromwell, on the site of an earlier castle. (Photograph: the authors)

Channel linked rather than separated the cultures of these areas. A contrasting example is the brick-building tradition introduced into the counties of central and eastern England in the later Middle Ages. Here, we find not only vernacular and parish-church building in brick, but also some castles, despite the obvious military disadvantages of this building material, including Caister-by-Norwich (Norfolk), Kirby Muxloe (Leicestershire) and Tattershall (Lincolnshire) (figure 50).

At Colchester (Essex) and Chepstow (Monmouthshire), Norman builders incorporated reused Roman tile into the exteriors of monumental donjons. Far from this simply reflecting a pragmatic recycling of building materials, in both cases it seems likely that conscious references were being made to the past for reasons of symbolism. At a far larger scale, the castle walls of Caernarfon, incorporating prominent polygonal towers and patterned with banded masonry, are thought to have been built in emulation of the tile-laced walls of Constantinople, emphasising the status of Edward I's great castle as an imposing icon of imperial ambition.

6
The wider contexts: castles, landscapes and townscapes

Major royal and urban castles apart, the overwhelming majority of British castles were centres of consumption and rural seats of lordship. Many castles also functioned as manorial centres. We often overlook the fact that most of these sites, whatever their defensive capabilities, had relatively mundane everyday lives as working farms closely linked to surrounding territories. British castles had a close association with the soil, and many were centred on prime agricultural areas. On a day-to-day basis, castle lords and their officials were concerned with the management of agricultural and other resources as well as with the collection of rents. It is thus unsurprising to find so many castles that are closely associated with features of the medieval agricultural landscape, such as watermills and field systems. Henry VIII's coastal artillery forts of the sixteenth century heralded a break in this long tradition, being the first major fortifications not to be integrated with their surrounding hinterlands.

In the countryside of England, Norman castles were inserted into rural landscapes where settlement patterns were often already well established, although in parts of Yorkshire and Durham the 'Harrying of the North' by William the Conqueror in 1069–70 had a devastating impact on settlement and economy. In parts of Celtic western Britain, castles were introduced as part of a new Norman package including nucleated villages, open field systems and a new form of manorial organisation. Occasionally, castles could have a disruptive effect on rural settlements, as at Rampton (Cambridgeshire), where an unfinished castle of unusual design was imposed on part of a village street, sealing houses and property boundaries. At Eaton Socon (Cambridgeshire), excavations have revealed the remains of a village and church that were obliterated during the castle's construction or development. More often, however, we see the positive effect of lordship on rural settlement through the creation of regular planned villages appended to castles, as at Castle Bolton (North Yorkshire), Laxton (Nottinghamshire) and Templeton (Pembrokeshire). The impact of castle-building on the village plan of Sheriff Hutton (North Yorkshire) was particularly pronounced given that it features two sites: a Norman fortification and a quadrangular castle of the fourteenth century, both of which are clearly related to episodes of settlement growth and replanning (figure 51). A more unusual example is Therfield (Hertfordshire), where a rectangular ditched and

51. The First Edition Ordnance Survey map of Sheriff Hutton, North Yorkshire (1895). The village contains the remains of two castles: at the east end of the settlement, adjacent to St Helen's church, can be identified those of a Norman castle ('mounds'); on the south side of the village lies its successor, the palatial late-fourteenth-century castle of the Neville family ('Sheriff Hutton Castle').

embanked enclosure attached to a small twelfth-century motte embraced the adjacent community and seems to have been built as an act of property protection during the turbulence of the anarchy in Stephen's reign.

Many other castles survive as apparently isolated features in the landscape. In some cases, these sites will have been originally associated with dependent villages or hamlets that have since been deserted or have migrated elsewhere. More (Shropshire) is a good example, where the castle lies on the fringe of a complex of earthworks representing peasant tenements and village streets; essentially similar examples include Kingerby (Lincolnshire), Whorlton (North Yorkshire) and Piperstown (Co. Louth). In areas of Britain where the medieval landscape was scattered with hamlets and farmsteads, as in Devon, many isolated castles were simply part and parcel of this dispersed settlement pattern. In the Vale of Montgomery, between Shrewsbury and the Welsh border, around ten miniature mottes were planted on the devastated estates of

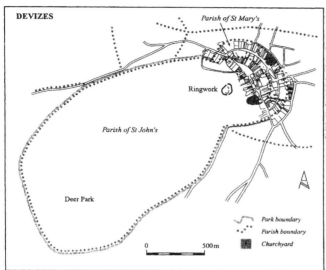

52. A plan of Devizes, Wiltshire, showing the location of the Bishop of Salisbury's castle between a large deer park and a planned medieval town with an unusual semicircular street plan. (Source: the authors)

the Earl of Shrewsbury in the 1070s to create a planned but non-nucleated settlement pattern to support the economic regeneration of the area.

Castles also show a clear link with hunting resources; a great number, such as Castle Camps (Cambridgeshire), Devizes (Wiltshire) (figure 52), Farleigh Hungerford (Somerset), Fotheringhay (Northamptonshire) and Stafford, were closely associated with enclosed private deer parks, enabling their aristocratic owners and guests to indulge their love of the chase, as well as providing a ready source of food and income. Castles in or near royal forests also doubled as hunting lodges – good examples being Ludgershall (Wiltshire) and Odiham (Hampshire) – and many were also the venues for forest courts and jails.

In addition to castles found in these many and varied rural locations, others formed parts of townscapes. Towns, of course, already had a long history of fortification. In Britain this went back to the Roman period, and even earlier Iron Age hillforts can be seen in the overall context of urban development. An essential contrast between defended towns and castles lay, however, in the communal nature of the former and the private nature of the latter. In some parts of Europe, especially the Mediterranean, we find aristocratic defensible residences within towns, whereas in Britain castle-building in an urban context (as opposed to those castles to which new planned towns were attached) was predominantly a royal phenomenon. This broad distinction was, however, occasionally blurred: in some Scottish and Irish towns defensible urban tower houses can be found, as for example at MacLellan's Castle

(Kirkcudbrightshire) and Taafe's Castle, Carlingford (Co. Louth).

As part of the Norman Conquest and its consolidation, castles were built systematically by William the Conqueror in important late Anglo-Saxon towns. Castle-building within these urban centres was a short-lived activity but with long-term consequences. A common location for these castles was an angle of existing defensive circuits of Roman and early medieval date – a policy making obvious military sense but often having disastrous results for the townsfolk. Good examples of this tradition include Canterbury (Kent), Chichester (West Sussex), Leicester, Totnes (Devon), Wareham (Dorset) and Winchester (Hampshire). At some of these sites, Domesday Book records the economic consequences of castle-building; at Lincoln, for instance, no fewer than 166 houses were said to have been destroyed. The impact of castle-building on the townscape of York was particularly pronounced given that here two complementary castles were erected, causing the disruption of settlement and the flooding of agricultural land to create the moated defences around the site later known as Clifford's Tower. In Winchester (Hampshire) (figure 53), the Norman castle was imposed over some of

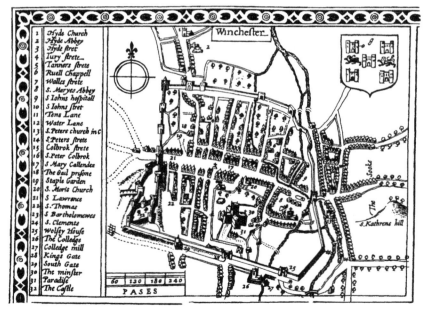

53. Winchester, Hampshire, as depicted in the early seventeenth century by John Speed. The royal castle occupied the south-west corner of the Roman city walls.

54. An aerial view of Warkworth, Northumberland, showing the medieval town planned at the foot of the castle. Located entirely within a loop of the River Coquet, the town plan is substantially medieval and individual burgage plots are still visible. (Crown copyright, NMR, English Heritage)

the Saxon street network, parts of which have been excavated underneath its earthworks, while at Wallingford (Oxfordshire), the town gate was re-sited and a road realigned to make way for an extension of the castle in the thirteenth century. Although such castles initially had important military functions, many were short-lived. For instance, the first Norman castle at Gloucester, squeezed into the south-west corner of the Roman city defences, was abandoned in favour of a fresh waterfront site in the early decades of the twelfth century. Though founded in military circumstances in the eleventh century, in subsequent centuries royal urban castles were more important for their judicial, financial and other administrative roles, in addition to their common proximity to royal forests.

Wales, Scotland and Ireland were essentially non-urban countries on the eve of the Norman Conquest, although in Ireland the foundation of

Viking coastal trading centres had led to some urban development, including defence, at Dublin and a few other places. In these areas, therefore, when Norman influence spread between the late eleventh and late twelfth centuries, castle and town foundations were often closely linked. In later contexts, too, castles and towns together were instruments of colonisation, as is especially evident in North Wales, where most of Edward I's castles, including Caernarfon (Gwynedd), Conwy (Conwy), Flint (Flintshire) and Rhuddlan (Denbighshire), were accompanied by grid-plan towns.

Paired castles and 'new towns' were complementary units, reflecting lordly interests accompanied by commercial activity. Urban foundation of this sort was also part of a wider European phenomenon, reflecting buoyant economic conditions. Throughout the British Isles the foundation of 'new towns' from the late eleventh century onwards was sometimes associated with, and often prompted by, seigneurial castle-building, as at Kidwelly (Carmarthenshire), Plympton (Devon), Tickhill (South Yorkshire) and Warkworth (Northumberland) (figure 54). The patrons of these new towns included secular and ecclesiastical lords and sometimes kings. The topographical relationship between castles and nascent towns took a variety of forms. Some towns, such as Bridgnorth (Shropshire), Richmond (North Yorkshire) and Trowbridge (Wiltshire), grew up within enclosed precincts appended to castles. Others, such as Corfe (Dorset), simply grew up around a market-place at the castle gate and were never themselves defended. Other examples, such as Ludlow (Shropshire) and New Radnor (Powys), assumed more economically inspired gridded layouts of regular form and were enclosed with their own walls and gates. Although many such places survived and flourished, others withered away, surviving now as earthworks and ruins in apparently rural situations. Among the best examples of these abortive plantations is Kilpeck (Herefordshire), now more famous for its remarkable parish church. Adjacent to this site can be identified an embanked settlement unit containing vestiges of medieval property boundaries. Other examples of failed castle towns include Almondbury (West Yorkshire), Castle Carlton (Lincolnshire) and the fascinating site of Kenfig (Glamorgan), where urban settlement formerly attendant to the castle lies buried beneath a dunefield.

7
Past, present and future

Given that the sites considered in this book display such a diverse range of plan, size, function, date and longevity, we might wonder whether the word 'castle' itself actually tells us very much. It is important to give careful consideration to archaeological and historical evidence about any particular site and not to have preconceptions about what a castle was and how it appeared and functioned. What is certain is that the impacts of castles on the landscapes and townscapes of Britain could be profound and enduring. The street patterns of countless modern towns and cities reflect the perimeters of former castle sites and settlements associated with them. The long curving market-place in the Wiltshire market town of Devizes, for instance, reflects the establishment of a commercial zone at the foot of the castle in the Norman period. Paradoxically, castles whose lifespans were short could still remain as permanent features of their surroundings: there is no simple correspondence between the longevity of a site's use and its legacy to the local landscape.

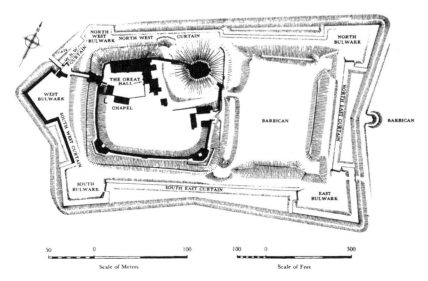

55. Carisbrooke Castle, Isle of Wight, showing the medieval castle surrounded by large angled bastions added in the late sixteenth century to a design of Frederigo Genebelli, a leading Italian military engineer. (Source: A. D. Saunders, *Fortress Britain*, 1989)

56. Carlisle, Cumbria, showing curtain wall, gatehouse and donjon, all altered for warfare in the age of gunpowder. (Photograph: the authors)

As the foregoing discussions will have made clear, castle design and use continued to evolve throughout the medieval period. Every generation developed new ideas about castle-building, either through the construction of new sites or, more commonly, the redevelopment of old castles. This evolution did not end with the so-called 'decline' of castles, traditionally ascribed in England and Wales to the Tudor period. Indeed, new castles, in the form of tower houses, were still being built in Ireland in the early seventeenth century and, in a wider sense, castles continued to be invented and reinvented up to the present day. Sites in certain locations saw ongoing military use. In the sixteenth century, some castles, including Carisbrooke (Isle of Wight) (figure 55), were upgraded through the provision of large earthen bastions for artillery, or, as at Carlisle (Cumbria), through the reduction of walls and modification of wall walks for the provision of cannon. Indeed, this castle continued to play a military role on the English–Scottish border well into modern times. It was attacked by the Jacobites in the 1745 rebellion and its barracks were occupied into the twentieth century (figure 56). Other sites were subjected to Civil War sieges in the 1640s, such as Old Basing (Hampshire) and Carew (Pembrokeshire), which were both upgraded with artillery bastions. At various points in the eighteenth, nineteenth and twentieth centuries, medieval castles were again called into use when national security was threatened. Pevensey Castle, for instance, was refortified in the Second World War with the addition of a pillbox. The military significance of Dover Castle (Kent) extended into the Cold War era, when it was refitted as a regional seat of government in the event of a nuclear war.

The architecture and social functions of medieval castles also had influence for a long time and over a wide area. The great country houses of the seventeenth to twentieth centuries were, in a social sense, the castles of their day. They represented wealth, status and contemporary architectural sophistication no less than had the castles of earlier centuries. Despite a lack of defences, their continued high status meant that the use of the word 'castle', sometimes applied to them by their builders, was perhaps more appropriate than is now commonly recognised. Conversely, many earlier castles had been the country seats of their aristocratic owners in the medieval period. In the post-medieval era, several distinct architectural trends of castle reinvention can be identified. The designs of buildings such as Bolsover Castle (Derbyshire), radically rebuilt in the seventeenth century, were inspired by the contemporary fashion for classical architecture. In sharp contrast, the almost fairy-tale qualities of William Burges's Castell Coch (Glamorgan), built in the 1880s on the foundations of a medieval castle, owe far more to the contemporary passion for the Gothic style than they did to the site's medieval appearance (figure 57). Even in the twentieth century, the image of the castle did not entirely disappear from architectural thinking. Commonly regarded as the last English castle, the sombre granite structure of Castle Drogo, Devon (designed by Sir Edwin Lutyens and started in 1911), was the home of a family whose wealth derived from commerce rather than from the landed estates that

57. Castell Coch, Glamorgan. (Photograph: the authors)

mainly supported castle-building in the medieval period (figure 58).

Castles were among the earliest monuments to be taken into state care and given protection through legislation. Conservation programmes were soon pursued both by public authorities and private owners. Notable pre-1914 works include Bodiam (Sussex), Caernarfon (Gwynedd) and Tattershall (Lincolnshire). At the start of the twenty-first century, the care and preservation of castles continues to flourish in the modern heritage industry. Moreover, the global significance of Britain's castle heritage received official recognition through the elevation in status of the 'Castles and Town Walls of King Edward in Gwynedd' and 'Durham Castle and Cathedral' and the 'Tower of London', all of which became World Heritage Sites between 1986 and 1988. Notably, these castle sites were not valued in isolation, but within the wider context of their built environments.

Above and beyond this use of castle sites as visual and educational reminders of our medieval heritage, they continue to be used as a valuable resource in a variety of other ways. Indeed, a small number of castles continue to fulfil some of their medieval social and political functions to the present day. Caernarfon Castle (Gwynedd), for instance, is the traditional venue for the investiture of the Prince of Wales. Exeter and Lancaster Castles are still the sites of law courts, reflecting the original status of royal urban castles as judicial centres. Some private castles continue in use as the hereditary seats of aristocratic families, including Alnwick (Northumberland; the Dukes of Northumberland), Arundel (West Sussex; the Dukes of Norfolk) and Belvoir (Leicestershire; the Earls of Rutland). Finally, and most famously, Windsor Castle (Berkshire) is still a royal residence more than nine hundred years after its establishment by William the Conqueror.

Presenting the physical remains of castles to the general public poses a number of challenges that have been dealt with in various ways, with varying levels of success. In the early twentieth century, castles, like monasteries, were the subject of careful clearance operations in which fallen masonry and overburdens of vegetation were systematically removed in order to expose the essentials of a site's plan. Subsequently, more refined methods were applied. These involved analysis and discovery of less obvious fabric and its display to the public. Sometimes such operations, particularly from the 1960s onwards, were also accompanied by extensive excavation and recording of standing remains by drawing and photography. Classic examples of this mode of investigation include Launceston (Cornwall), Okehampton (Devon), Castle Rising (Norfolk), Castle Acre (Norfolk), Sandal (West Yorkshire), Barnard Castle (Co. Durham) and Ludgershall (Wiltshire). These and other programmes produced the quintessentially British 'ancient'

58. Castle Drogo, Devon. (Photograph: the authors)

monument, with its meticulously cared for fabric, neat lawns and highly regulated, visitor-friendly environment. In such cases, the underlying philosophy was 'conserve as found', and only in exceptional cases was reconstruction of fabric undertaken. This extended even to the conservation *in situ* of heavily fragmented or even precarious masonry, as seen at Caerphilly Castle (Glamorgan), with its famous leaning tower.

By the 1990s, however, a modified approach to conservation had emerged. Intervention in the masonry remains of a site was kept to a bare minimum and vegetation cover restrained but not removed, as at Wigmore (Herefordshire). The effect has been to create a more 'natural' monument, in contrast to the more clinical approach of earlier years. Different challenges of conservation and presentation confront those responsible for castles that are still people's homes, such as Saltwood (Kent), including the need to reconcile the legitimate domestic needs of occupants with the demands of conservation and the laws that control it. In the modern era, many people's impressions of castles are as likely to be influenced by the depiction of these sites on film and television screen as by visiting them in person. For example, Alnwick and Bamburgh (Northumberland), Castell Coch (Glamorgan), Trim (Co. Meath), Wardour (Wiltshire) and others have provided the backdrops for dramas of one sort or another. This phenomenon is not, however, a new one. One of English cinema's earliest films, a production of *Ivanhoe*, was set within the ruins of Chepstow Castle (Monmouthshire) in 1913.

There is still much that we do not know about castles and their builders. Castle studies continue to evolve and show every sign of flourishing, and there are a number of promising avenues for future research in the field. First, there exists a major requirement for more extensive excavation of early castle baileys, particularly those associated with timber castles. We urgently need to know how the crucial evidence from Hen Domen (Powys) compares with other contemporary sites elsewhere within the British Isles. Second, studies of the architecture and domestic planning of eleventh- to fourteenth-century masonry castles have revealed the complex and fascinating ways in which space within buildings was used and manipulated. Further analysis in this mode is needed from a variety of sites widely distributed in time and space. Third, while detailed site-specific studies of these sorts have a major role to play in the future, equally important are analyses of the contribution of castles to medieval landscapes and townscapes. Fourth, historical studies have emphasised the symbolic significance of the licensing of castle building in the thirteenth to fifteenth centuries. This major advance needs supplementing with wider documentary and architectural study to establish the relative importance of status and defence in the development of late medieval castles. Fifth, and finally, as this book has made clear, castle studies open numerous avenues into the wider medieval world. With this in mind, greater attention should be given to integrating castle studies within the full framework of medieval scholarship. In particular, the fields of literary study, art history, critical theory, garden history and historical geography deserve increased attention alongside the more traditional fields of social, political, architectural and military history. Although the archaeological study of castles can certainly help to answer broad historical questions, by their very nature the physical and environmental data that archaeologists confront are more appropriate to an understanding of everyday life. Somewhat frustrating is the fact that archaeology can fall short of dating sites and their development with the degree of precision that documentary historians deem desirable. Conversely, excavation and building analysis can be rich sources of information about medieval social and economic life, on which documentary sources are so often silent.

8
Sites to visit

There are more than a thousand castle sites of diverse types and dates in England and Wales. Large numbers of these are accessible to visitors, either as managed sites in the hands of public agencies or privately owned sites where visiting is permitted. It is, however, impossible to provide a comprehensive list of places to visit. Readers should note that: (a) the mention of a site within this book does not necessarily imply access to the public; and (b) visitors must respect the legally protected status of most castles as Scheduled Ancient Monuments. The following list comprises simply a selection of sites, balanced in terms of date, location and type. An asterisk (*) indicates sites with free public access; all others are managed by private or public agencies and charge entry fees. Ownership by English Heritage is denoted by the letters EH; NT denotes sites owned by the National Trust; ownership by Cadw of castle sites in Wales is also indicated. These organisations have websites from which more information can be obtained (www.english-heritage.org.uk; www.nationaltrust.org.uk; www.cadw.wales.gov.uk). The National Grid Reference is given for each site.

England
Almondbury, West Yorkshire. SE 153141. (The earthwork remains of a de Lacy castle with associated settlement; within a hillfort.)

Beeston, Cheshire. SJ 537593. EH. Telephone: 01829 260464. (The thirteenth-century castle of the Earls of Chester; on a prominent rock in the Cheshire plain.)

Bodiam, East Sussex. TQ 785256. NT. Telephone: 01580 830196. (A late-fourteenth-century prestige building in landscaped and moated surrounds.)

**Castle Acre*, Norfolk. TF 819151. EH. (A country house of the de Warenne family; transformed into a castle in the twelfth century.)

Castle Rising, Norfolk. TF 666246. EH. Telephone: 01553 631330. (An ornate Norman donjon surrounded by massive ringworks partly burying the church.)

Colchester, Essex. TL 999253. Telephone: 01206 282932. Website: www.colchestermuseums.org.uk (A massive Norman royal donjon built on Roman foundations; the upper storey has been removed.)

Corfe Castle, Dorset. SY 959823. NT. Telephone: 01929 481294. (A spectacularly sited royal castle on a hilltop commanding the Isle of Purbeck.)

Dover, Kent. TR 325418. EH. Telephone: 01304 211067. (A strategically crucial royal fortress maintained over many centuries.)

**Edlingham*, Northumberland. NU 116092. EH. (The excavated remains of a manor house upgraded to a castle in the later medieval period.)

Goodrich, Herefordshire. SO 577200. EH. Telephone: 01600 890538. (A Norman donjon surrounded by the replanned castle of the early fourteenth century.)

**Hallaton*, Leicestershire. SP 780967. (The small but impressive earthworks of a motte and bailey never rebuilt in stone.)

Kenilworth, Warwickshire. SP 278723. EH. Telephone: 01926 852078. (A Norman castle transformed into a palatial residence amidst complex water features.)

**Kilpeck*, Herefordshire. SO 444305. (A Norman motte and failed borough with a parish church famous for sculptures.)

Launceston, Cornwall. SX 331846. EH. Telephone: 01566 772365. (The Earl of Cornwall's castle, well known for its profile of a dual stone tower on a motte.)

**Laxton*, Nottinghamshire. SK 720676. (A well-preserved motte and bailey in a village famous for its partly surviving open fields.)

London: the Tower. TQ 336805. Telephone: 0870 756 6060 (infoline). Website: www.hrp.org.uk (William the Conqueror's urban palace-donjon built in the corner of the Roman city.)

**Lydford*, Devon. SX 509848 and SX 508847. EH. (The adjacent Norman fort and later stannary prison-tower within the Saxon town defences.)

**Nunney*, Somerset. ST 737458. EH. (The new fourteenth-century castle comprising a residential tower surrounded by a moat.)

**Odiham*, Hampshire. SU 725518. (An early-thirteenth-century royal castle and hunting lodge centred on a tower with an octagonal plan.)

Okehampton, Devon. SX 583942. EH. Telephone: 01837 52844. (A Norman castle with a large motte; rebuilt in the fourteenth century with major domestic ranges.)

Old Sarum, Wiltshire. SU 137327. EH. Telephone: 01722 335398. (A bishop's castle built in an enormous ringwork, with a cathedral, in an Iron Age hillfort.)

Old Wardour, Wiltshire. ST 938263. EH. Telephone: 01747 870487. (The new, late-fourteenth-century octagonal tower in a later landscaped setting.)

Orford, Suffolk. TM 419498. EH. Telephone: 01394 450472. (An unusual twelfth-century royal donjon, formerly surrounded by masonry outer defences.)

**Pilsbury*, Derbyshire. SK 114638. (Clearly preserved motte and baileys situated in the bottom of the Dove valley.)

**Plympton*, Devon. SX 544558. (A large motte with fragmentary shell keep showing the remains of timber reinforcement.)

Portchester, Hampshire. SU 624046. EH. Telephone: 023 9237 8291. (A royal castle, comprising donjon and bailey, in a corner of a Roman Saxon Shore fort.)

Restormel, Cornwall. SX 104614. EH. Telephone: 01208 872687. (A late-thirteenth-century shell keep with masonry domestic ranges; on a Norman earthwork.)

Rochester, Kent. TQ 741686. EH. Telephone: 01634 402276. (A famous twelfth-century donjon noted for its height and internal Romanesque detail.)

**Sandal*, West Yorkshire. SE 337181. Telephone: 01924 249779. (A Norman earth-and-timber castle later rebuilt in stone on a massive scale.)

**Skipsea*, East Yorkshire. TA 162551. EH. (An imposing Norman motte standing in a former mere, with an adjacent failed borough.)

Warkworth, Northumberland. NU 247058. EH. Telephone: 01665 711423. (A motte and bailey, redeveloped with a unique fourteenth-century donjon and collegiate church.)

York: Clifford's Tower. SE 605515. Telephone: 01904 646940. (A Norman motte with a thirteenth-century quatrefoil-planned donjon of unusual design.)

Wales

Beaumaris, Anglesey. SH 607763. Cadw. Telephone: 01248 810361. (The last and most concentrically planned of Edward I's castles in Wales; unfinished.)

Caernarfon, Gwynedd. SH 477627. Cadw. Telephone: 01286 677617. (The centrepiece of Edward I's castle-building in Wales; accompanied by a planned town.)

Caerphilly, Glamorgan. ST 155871. Cadw. Telephone: 029 2088 3143. (A thirteenth-century baronial castle with elements of concentricity; has extensive water features.)

Cardiff, Glamorgan. ST 180767. Telephone: 029 2087 8100. (A motte with shell keep, built within a Roman fort; extensively restored in the nineteenth century.)

Castell Coch, Glamorgan. ST 131826. Cadw. Telephone: 029 2081 0101. (A late-nineteenth-century neo-Gothic building on the foundations of a triangular thirteenth-century castle.)

Chepstow, Monmouthshire. ST 533941. Cadw. Telephone: 01291 624065. (A Norman hall, with Roman masonry, modified in the thirteenth century; has extensive baileys.)

Conwy, Conwy. SH 784775. Cadw. Telephone: 01492 592358. (An Edwardian multi-towered fortress with royal apartments and a walled borough.)

Criccieth, Gwynedd. SH 500377. Cadw. Telephone: 01766 522227. (The early-thirteenth-century castle of Llywelyn, later redeveloped by both the Welsh and the English.)

*Dolforwyn, Powys. SO 152950. Cadw. (An extensive thirteenth-century Welsh castle and borough; later occupied by the English.)

Harlech, Gwynedd. SH 581313. Cadw. Telephone: 01766 780552. (An Edwardian castle on a rock outcrop; planned employing concentric principles.)

Laugharne, Carmarthenshire. SN 302107. Cadw. Telephone: 01994 427906. (A thirteenth-century double enclosure with towers; much added to in the sixteenth century.)

*Montgomery, Powys. SO 221968. Cadw. (A Welsh border castle founded by Henry III in the 1220s; on a rocky spur near the River Severn.)

Pembroke, Pembrokeshire. SM 982016. Telephone: 01646 684585. (A marcher lordship castle and town; with a round donjon built by William Marshall *c*.1200.)

Raglan, Monmouthshire. SO 415083. Cadw. Telephone: 01291 690228. (A fifteenth-century castle on an earlier site; with a moated donjon and extensive domestic ranges.)

Tretower, Powys. SO 184212. Cadw. Telephone: 01874 730279. (A motte and bailey with shell keep and round donjon; a later manor house is adjacent.)

Further reading

For the researcher interested in tackling the history or archaeology of a specific castle, an important reference work is D.J. Cathcart King's magisterial two-volume *Castellarium Anglicanum* (Kraus International, 1983), which comprises an extensive index of castles in England and Wales, along with an invaluable annotated bibliography. Other useful lists of published material relating to castle sites are contained within J.R. Kenyon's comprehensive *Castles, Town Defences and Artillery Fortifications in the United Kingdom and Ireland: A Bibliography 1945-2006* (Shaun Tyas, 2008). Other readily available sources of information on individual sites are the county volumes of the *Victoria County History of England*, the inventories of the *Royal Commissions* in England, Scotland and Wales, and the 'Buildings of England' series written by N. Pevsner, and latterly Bridget Cherry. Many articles concerning the archaeology and architectural development of castles are published in journals or periodicals including the *Castle Studies Group Journal*, *Archaeological Journal*, and *Medieval Archaeology*, and other material arising from conferences, such as the *Proceedings of the Battle Conferences on Anglo-Norman Studies*, and the publications of the biennial *Château Gaillard* colloquia. The following list comprises only selected books and monographs.

Early Studies

Armitage, E.S. *The Early Norman Castles of the British Isles*. Murray, 1912.
Clark, G. T. *Mediaeval Military Architecture in England*. Wyman, 1884–85. Two volumes.
Hamilton Thompson, A. *Military Architecture in England During the Middle Ages*. Oxford University Press, 1912.

General Studies

Brown, R.A. *English Castles*. Batsford, 1976.
Goodall, J. *The English Castle, 1066-1650*. Yale University Press, 2011.
Johnson, M. *Behind the Castle Gate: Medieval to Renaissance*. Routledge,2002.
Kenyon, J. and O'Conor, K. (editors) *The Medieval Castle in Ireland and Wales*. Four Courts Press, 2003.
Kenyon, J.R. *Medieval Fortifications*. Leicester University Press, 1990.
Liddiard, R. *Castles in Context: Power, Symbolism and Landscape, 1066 to 1500*. Windgather, 2005.
McNeill, T. *Castles in Ireland: Feudal Power in a Gaelic World*. Routledge, 1997.
Platt, C. *The Castle in Medieval England and Wales*. Chancellor, 1995.
Pounds, N.J.G. *The Medieval Castle in England and Wales: A Social and Political History*. Cambridge University Press, 1990.
Sweetman, D. *The Medieval Castles of Ireland*. Collins, 2000.
Tabraham, C. *Scottish Castles and Fortifications*. HMSO, 1986.
Thompson, M.W. *The Decline of the Castle*. Cambridge University Press, 1987.

Early Castles
Higham, R.A. and Barker, R.A. *Timber Castles*. Batsford, 1992.
Thompson, M.W. *The Rise of the Castle*. Cambridge University Press, 1991.
Renn, D. *Norman Castles in Britain*. John Baker, 1968.

Warfare
Bradbury, J. *The Medieval Siege*. Boydell, 1992.
Saunders, A.D. *Fortress Britain: Artillery Forts in the British Isles and Ireland*. Beaufort, 1989.

Castles and Landscapes
Creighton, O.H. *Castles and Landscapes*. Equinox, 2005.
Creighton, O.H. *Designs upon the Land: Elite Landscapes of the Middle Ages*. Boydell, 2009.

Excavation Reports
Austin, D. *Acts of Perception: A Study of Barnard Castle in Teesdale*. Architectural and Archaeological Society of Durham and Northumberland, 2007.
Beresford, G. *Goltho: The Development of an Early Medieval Manor c. 850–1150*. HMSO, 1987.
Ellis, P. (editor) *Ludgershall Castle, Wiltshire: A Report on the Excavations by Peter Addyman, 1964–1972*. Wiltshire Archaeological and Natural History Society monograph number 2, 2000.
Higham, R.A. and Barker, P.A. *Hen Domen, Montgomery. A Timber Castle on the English-Welsh Border: A Final Report*. University of Exeter Press, 2000.

Building and Documentary Studies
Emery, A. *Greater Medieval Houses of England and Wales, 1300-1500*. Cambridge: Cambridge University Press, 1996-2006. Three volumes.
Impey, E. *The White Tower*. Yale University Press, 2008.

Index

Page numbers in italic refer to illustrations.